Odds & Ends

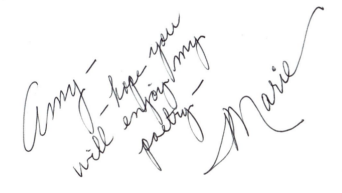

by

Marie Puckett

Odds & Ends

Library of Congress
Cataloging in Publication Data

ISBN 1-58235-952-0

Manufactured in The United States of America by
Watermark Press
6 Gwynns Mill Court
Owings Mills, MD 21117
410-654-0400

Black & White

For Gary and Millie Stewart

A newspaper......
A graph... A T.V....
Salt and pepper are that too.

Black is sadness,
White is purity.
Black is night,
White is light.

The combination is you see,
A fulfillment of your love for me.

1974

Tryfenie

Away the cobwebs fell from my mind's eye.
It had been years since I had memory of "try".
Elegant, tall, lean and quite lovely was try.

I met her one Sunday in Baltimore,
she had invited me to dinner.
And what a dinner, roast beef, rice all very nice.
We had drinks and talked afterwards.
She started looking for something to give me as
as a token to remember her.
My gift in the end was an item from India,
a miniature coffee urn.
I wish I could say I still had it,
but it was misplaced over the years.
I will always remember her kindness

May 1995

Gathering Nature

A golden moon hanging on a still ebony lake.
Has the effect of being aged on canvas for years.
The cracks of the canvas are tiny ripples on the lake.
How still the sound, how still the wind, how still the leaves.

Up the lake come two floating figures, on large loon,
and his mate, singing that crazy sound only they can make.
More action on the lake since it is dawn.
A few deer having their morning drink.

We have to be moving on our time here is through.
On to another spot in another place to gather pictures.
Pictures of the mind, that will stay forever.
Pictures of the lens that will stay.

April 1995

Marie Puckett

Always Looking

Searching the silky white clouds every morning.
Searching the blue-gray clouds each evening.
Looking at all the cloud formations for a sign.
Looking at the trees for small changes,
listening to the song of the birds.
Listening to the babbling brooks sing.
Gazing at the smiling faces of young children,
Going back to the sunshine thro' the clouds,
for my last long look—-
Trying to see the Lord—-coming!!!!!

The mountain top
June 22, 1995

Salty Tales

Sounds from the far off shore, telling their tale
high pitches shrieking sounds of the dead,
telling of loves gone by, of lost loves of Galway Bay.
Captains of ships gone out to sea, never to return.
Outrageous treasures given up to the bottom of the sea.
Voices from the tips of foam from a distant wave,
singing the sailors prayer, to all who would listen.

It is as if we who stand here listening will hear a message,
just for us, a message from the deep.
How lonely it must be year after year alone!!!!!

Marble Inn
April 17, 1995

Marie Puckett

Somewhere, somehow, my time will be,
somewhere, sometime, a place,
for you and me, for somewhere
sometime my love for you will grow,
and some day you will be here,
somewhere, somehow, sometime......

Listen To My Soul

I hear a soft whisper, a very soft and sweet one.
A long time it had been silent not a sound from it.
I often wondered if my soul were male or female,
while we were on good terms my soul was soft and kind.
While it was silent it seemed so hard and cold.
Kind and soft is female and cold and hard is male.

My soul aches for sweet love and contentment,
I shall give her this and more in my hour of bliss.

July 2, 1996, South-Kornor

Fireflies

Playing in the yard,
running barefoot on the lawn.
Chasing the fireflies for your very own.

Watching them glitter and light up the night,
like thousands of candles they flicker in flight.

Someone is wearing a brand new ring,
the children are laughing.
Oh! Hear them sing.

Someone is wearing a necklace of bright beads.
So many fireflies have died for these deeds.

January 3, 1981

Eyes

Mysterious, warm, bright, cheerful, sad—
This describes the eyes both good and bad—
Green eyes, belong to the Irish with blazing hair of red.
Brown eyes, to the Italians, hot blooded and bold.
Blue eyes, to the English, with pomp and circumstance,
Hazel eyes, to the Gypsies, who love and love and dance.
Black eyes, to India the people old and true.

All eyes are awake to the dawn,
and sing the dance of the fawn.

July 18, 1984

Marie Puckett

Sunday Mornings

Coffee, juice, newspaper funnies
Complete the Sunday morning.

I waking you, you kissing me –
What a wonderful way to set your heart singing.

Leisurely sipping our coffee –
Making some little "small talk"

Thinking of changing from pj's to shorts
and going to the park for our walk.

Of course taking Lord Grey and Lady Faye –

Just another Sunday –
Passing our way.

July 13, 1989

Lord Grey And Lady Faye

My lovely male and female cats –
How wonderful to see the affection
they have for each other.

She is so feminine, to him, her
Lord Grey.

He is content to wait
on Lady Faye.

So handsome is he and she
so fair.

She would follow him,
to the ends of the world,
to anywhere!

August 30, 1989

Tears

Tears of joy –
Tears of sorrow –
Tears from fears about tomorrow.

Falling droplets of water
Caused by many feelings,
births, weddings, graduations, deaths
are times when tears are shed
by those with many understandings.

December 30, 1981

Love

Love...a much used word.
Love...a much misused word.
Used by some to gain control,
of those who would sell their soul.

Used by others who know too well
the sadness of people who will not tell.

Love is used, very sad but true.
Not often enough by those who do.

Used by some who would never stop to think
why they've waiting so long to tell someone on the brink –
of love.

1978

Shades Of Blue

Indigo, sky blue, royal and peacock,
shades of blue, a painted rock.

Navy, baby, teal, and aqua
brilliant blues from Samartra.

Jungle blues, oriental shades
Winter blues, summer blues
Springs rippling glades

All warm the soul
and keep the earth aglow.

December 30, 1981

Our Love Song

True love never runs smooth,
or so they say –
Our love should have lasted,
come what may.
We waited so long for one another,
everyone could see how much we cared.
True – our love was deep and strong.
So! – Dear God! How could it go wrong.
I was so true to you, and I thought you knew,
how much I cared for you.
You loved me with all your heart –
It's hard to believe we are apart.
We've done something wrong,
and it's too late, for our love song.

Turbulent Sea

Sunshine, carefree days,
good luck coming to me in hundreds
of ways.
Everything going my way,
I knew it would last to the very last days.
Oh! How easy it is to fool one's self,
that this would last forever.
It seemed as tho the gods turned
their backs on me.
And I thought – Oh! - never.
All my joys became sorrow.
I dared to hope! Would there be a tomorrow?
And then blessings of blessings,
God sent you to me.
My life had been headed for deep water; you see
But now I have my anchor in the
turbulent sea.
My dearest, I know it's your love for me

1991

Imperial Shores

Before the God, was God –
Pebbles washed up from the sea,
as gems, of jade, as green as the tea.
Sunlight danced on them.
Birds perched on them and sang.
They glistened with the salt of the sea.
Calm were the shores,
on which were seen the most glorious sunsets.
Great king turtles swam,
and in great abundance fished.
Peace was profound.
Peace covered the earth without sound.
Sands of the beach sparkled like millions of diamonds,
on this the imperial shore.
Days and half days were all that were,
sea storms were in the far future,
when man would govern the Imperial Shores.

1992

Marie Puckett

She Is –

Brass cat sitting on the pyramid of Hyrogliphirs,
How proud, how silent, how god-like is she.
She is regal in her pomp and circumstance.
All at curt bow low before her.
Her life began well before the time of coming.
The spirit of Amana, the Brass Cat is in everyone.
All who believe must show strength,
all must be obedient to Amana.
At nite Amana leaves her throne
and walks the night of Kra.
Kra, her spirit love of all ages,
still consumes her, over history's pages.

1992

Mom

When I was young, you were near and dear.
But something happened with each passing year.
Your love for me seemed to drift away.
Like so much foam on the ocean spray.
I seemed to have been left behind;
as so many trinkets very hard to find.
Then for a very short time we became close
I went away and our love increased with a great force.
Mom, now that you're gone, I need you so,
each year that passes makes me – love you more.
I must be content in knowing that,
one day we will embrace and be together again.

1983

Yesterday

Warm sunshine on my face –
Wonderful!
Soft white sand beneath my feet –
Wonderful!
Salt water waves stinging my cheeks.
On vacation for three weeks!
Exciting beach parties.
Wonderful!
A feast of lobster, shrimp and clams
I felt like a youngster at Christmas.
Met several people, who became friends
wonderful!
Relaxation was my number one goal.
Oh! for the joy of it all.
But that was yesterday.

1991

A Cloud For Aldo

White clouds on a deep purple sea,
my eyes see this at first glance.
To my surprise the clouds are sails.
Sails on a small fishing boat.
How often he had painted this scene.
The sea, sky and white sails.
Changing the overcast sky to blue,
the stormy sea to a calm one.
but the boat and sail – always the same.
Always going out to sea –
Going out until the sail becomes a cloud afloat.

2000

Marie Puckett

An Indian Summer

A wonderful bright sunshine morning
With a robin-egg blue sky.
Along with a lovely slight breeze.
A few white fluffy clouds.
Dancing slowly overhead.
Red and golden leaves fall
swiftly from my trees.
Four gray squirrels, residents of the block
go scampering up and down the trees.
And run the sidewalks and lawns.
This is my favorite time of the year.
Wish it could stay, as it leaves I give a cheer.

1998

Mice

I love large stuffed mice,
wearing pointy hats with bells.
And tiny ones with twisted tails.
To hang upon a Christmas tree.
And still others mounted on tea pots.
As quaint as quaint can be.
Mice make cute silver earrings and bobs.
Artistic fellows doing fine jobs.
Cut tiny caricatures on posted notes.
Perk up an otherwise gloomy day.
But when it comes to wiggly loves ones,
they just plain scare me.

1998

Marie Puckett

The Birth

Giving birth in safety,
furnishing shelter and warm bed.
Warm fresh milk, an unending supply.
Supervised play and exercise;
all this given with much love.
Add a proper bath every day.
You may think the above be human kind.
But no – I speak of the animal kingdom in Africa.

Soul Mate

In the darkest of darkness,
I thought I had never had a soul mate.
Reading of them, hearing about them.
How wonderful to experience one.
Time passes and I now know of several.
One true love at age sixteen –
Who in spirit has stayed with me.
When I was lost and found.
I was in need he stayed with me.
And my greatest of late – Aldo,
my deepest love and so,
you see I now have more than one.

1998

Marie Puckett

We Have A Son

We decided not to learn if the babe be a girl or a boy.
So, we waited and with each passing month –
The list of names grew and selecting a name a joy.
If it would be a boy all the names were of the Bible and strong.
Girls names seemed to be for us more difficult.
The day finally came, it's a boy –
A lovely beautiful strong boy.
And his chosen name is Josiah.

1995

Something Blue

A Christmas wedding is so special,
to think you will be wed to the one you truly love.
On the day Christ's birth is celebrated.
Mother of the bride busily makes dresses for the bridesmaids.
Ideas of the dresses and capes with muffs were all in her mind.
Dresses must be made before the memory fades.
All were finished for the final fitting.
Two in dark forest green and two in berry-red.
Now for the bride, her gown and train –
Both will be finished in ecru tone old fashioned lace.
Oh! my we have forgotten something,
a much different color than above.
A garter of satin, in blue from mom with love.

1993

Seashore—at Cape Cod

Sounds are the first thing to marvel.
Such a clamor of busy conversation, coming from the gulls.
You wonder if the Tower of Babel could compare.
This beautiful white feathered community feed, make friends.
And in the end produce more gulls to join their symphony.
Clean fresh salty ocean air,
long lasting colorful sunsets,
not to outdo the sunrise.
Busy little pink flowers coming thru the fine-
small white cottages dot the shoreline.
Old and new wooden boats dot the sand.
Collecting sea shells could be a full time job.
So many shells, not one of a kind.
Once one is in your grasp, you can't let go.
Being outdoors all day, builds an appetite.
A clam bake at night – a pure delight.
Sounds of waves at midnight.

Lake Kincaid, 1993

A Gift For Sarah

Sarah was so excited, she had won a trip to the city.
But sad, as momma could see,
Sarah had no special dress to wear,
to go to the city for her award.
A dress must be made and fast.
Everyone started finding things that would do.
Cranberry crepe from grandma's old Sunday dress.
Cut down for Sarah and trimmed in the very best,
black satin collar and cuffs,
from the lining of an old vest.
Old Irish lace, to trim the collar and cuffs,
from grandma's old, odd pillow case.
A belt was made and a rhinestone buckle found.
Looking at Sarah's dress in our mind's eye,
we can tell all is well.

1993

Marie Puckett

Old Fashion Flowers

Sounds of the break of dawn.
The milkman cometh and so do the iceman.
Flowers neatly placed in rows of four or more.
In lovely handpainted window boxes
painted with ethnic designs of white, red and green,
the strong sturdy geraniums, the old world flower.
Every year the women of East 71st Street.
Tenderly put bright pinks and deep reds out on parade.
Seeing these flowers parade year after year, is quite a treat.

July 16, 1992

Children's Laughter

Children's laughter ever sounding –
Heals my heart and sets it pounding,
with joys of joys unending!

Their laughter is true and loveable –
Oh! how their eyes sparkle.
Their laughter resounding
causes us to chuckle.

Children all aglow with the spirit of love,
each one knowing what love and life is all about.

1978

Lovers And Friends

How we perceive ourselves
as lovers and friends,

It depends –

When friends become lovers,
he receives the message
she sends.

He answers and waits for her reply,
he pretends.

She goes forward –
and friends become lovers,
she contends.

September 4, 1989

"Attila"

"Attila"...King of the Huns,
Giant of giants...seven feet tall.
Strong...weak...fierce...kind.
Attila father of all.

Our tale begins on a warm balmy night,
his mother is waiting, his father is gone.
Campfires dance around black pots.
A doe and a buck come into camp with a fawn.

Riders approach at the break of dawn.
The camp's in a bustle, what a crowd to feed.
Women are expected to cook the stew,
this will be some great deed.

Back in the main tent, a son is born,
"Attila" by name.
The mother so frail dies in childbirth.
His father returns from a great hunt,
all the camp is filled with sadness and mirth.

Hungarian celebration of birth and death
lasts for months.
Dancers dance 'til out of breath.
"Attila's" father leaves for other hunts,
the last hunt ending with Igor's death.

All the tribes are gathered,
first come the burial fires for Magda and Igor
attended by all the chieftains.
Women all wail sad laments,
children huddle in masses at their tents.

"Attila" three moons old is orphaned,
but not for long.
Zoe will care for him as her own.
She holds him close and sings her song –

"Attila"...King of the Huns,
giant of giants... seven feet tall.
Strong...weak...fierce...kind.
Attila father of all

Christmas Teddys

Under the tree we find,
all sorts of Teddys, not one of a kind.

Some are brown and very funny,
others are white with red bows and curly.

Still under a lovely pine,
sits a black Teddy, a friend of mine.

He seems to be the strongest of all,
but tender, and cuddly, sitting near a red ball.

All boys and girls give them names,
like Sammy, Annie, Sally and James.

Christmas Teddys are given with love,
and last for years as a warm memory.

1989

Christmas

Peanut butter cookies cooling on racks,
pizzelles standing on the table in stacks.

Pumpkin pies by the dozens –
Apple strudel just from the oven.

Turkey and dressing, cranberries too!
Santa unable to get thru the flue.

Children inspecting gifts under the tree,
birds, cats and dogs excited as we.

The aunts, uncles, nieces, nephews, and grandparents agree –
It's the birth of our Lord, Jesus Christ you see!

12/19/81

Christmas

C hrist is born this night

H is love shining oh! so bright

R ise and sing to our King

I n all the lands church bells ring

S hepherds tending their flocks

T ell us of a wondrous sight

M yrrh, frankincense, and gold are gifts

A t this holy time by three kings

S ilently expressing their love this season brings

December 19, 1989

The Picnic

Perfect Sunday weather in July
Hot dogs, chips and apple pie.

Grandma's spice cake, Aunt Jen's jello
Sally, Tom and Mello-Yellow.

Grandpa's horseshoes, Ken's baseball,
Dad's laughter, moms love for all.

Annie dancing merrilee
Harry's band, "The Jubilee"

Nightfall comes and fun begins
With fireworks set off by the Weatherly twins.

12/30/81

Awareness

The feeling of total awareness,
the understanding of the plan
set down for you alone.
Paths one must take though
some be difficult.
Decisions one makes after careful
thought.
Sights to be seen through only
your eyes.
Feelings only you can comprehend.
Compassion you feel for all
you see or hear about.
Your over abundance to love
and be loved.
Awareness coming from your soul.

12/4/74

Womanhood

A little girl is born
She is loved by everyone.
Years pass by, school beings.
She has many good times.
These years are short,
she grows into a beautiful, young lady
Filled with charm and grace.
She meets a young man –
A family begins.
Her children love her,
her husband is so proud.
The years slip away.
Now there are only two.
Just the little girl grown old
and her husband true.

12/30/81

Sandy

A girl with taffy hair –
She is a beauty beyond compare.
She is so sweet to see –
How I wish that I were she.

She laughs and makes the children sing.
For she is lovingly kind –
Such innocence you no longer find.

And who is this little dandy?
A friend of mine, her name is Sandy.

12/4/74

Alaska

A beautiful country, our land to the north,
so full of serenity and full of worth.

The peaceful countrysides, lakes and streams,
are dotted here and there with hidden dreams.

Once undisturbed by people and progress,
this land is filled with unexplored tundras,
which are in distress.

12/2/74

Africa

The golden land of opportunity calls
She is surrounded by ivory walls.

Her coasts of gold are filled with grief.
Her poor population are on relief.

She wastes so much that she could give.
Her children cry out and want to live.

To be the people only they can be,
free, healthy, rich in love for one another,
as it should be.

12/4/74

Marie Puckett

The Picnic

Perfect Sunday weather in July
Hot dogs, chips and apple pie.

Grandma's spice cake, Aunt Jen's jello
Sally, Tom and Mello-Yellow.

Grandpa's horseshoes, Ken's baseball,
Dad's laughter, moms love for all.

Annie dancing merrily
Harry's band, "The Jubilee"

Nightfall comes and fun begins
With fireworks set off by the Weatherly twins.

12/30/81

Books For Cats

Once upon a time, long ago a very tiny collection of books
sat on a tiny shelf in a very small cottage.
A small cat scampered over each book each day of the week,
each week of the month, each month of the year.
A wee gray mouse scampered over the books each day
of the week,
each week of the month and each month of the year.
Oh! What fun they had, they knew each book by sight.
The cat had her favorite, "Jack London", stories of ships at sea.
However the mouse was more content with, "The Good Earth,"
and all its fields to scamper through......

Marie Puckett

Sore Feet

Sore feet hurt don't 'cha know —-
Oh!! How they "bark" for you to get off your feet.
Buy a new pair of leather shoes, and wear them
the first time to church.
You come a squeakin' down the aisle with everyone
lookin' at you.
It's bad enough that the tie is tight and
the shirt is double starched,
But oh!! Them sore feet, hot as Hades, and blisters galore.
Tears come down your cheeks, someone says praise the Lord,
they think you have been blessed is the reason for the tears, if
they only knew about these sore, sore feet.

6/20/96

Tulips

Small dark brown bulbs,
planted underground
come bursting through
in the Spring with a bound.

Such brilliant colors
come forth to give
their lasting beauty
wherever they live.

In Holland, France, Texas or Spain
in gardens all over in small towns or plains.

Whether picked for the table,
potted or left,
their warmth will continue
until they are spent.

1/3/92

Marie Puckett

Passion

Closeness of two people whether young or old,
come about by being shy, maybe bold.

Sending gifts of flowers, cards and letters –
Gifts of ties, furs, rings and "cupie dolls" with feathers,

Seem to improve each other's knowledge of their feelings-
Feelings that grow completely out of proportion,
until both are consumed with passion.

Passion so strong they know its real
the "kind-of-stuff" you get with sex appeal.

Passion that gives you a glow –
So warm and lovely, like the moon on fresh fallen snow.

Time passes, after three or more years,
something happens, one takes the other for granted.

Doubt steps in; trust leaves,
the passion dies – is there more!

The Artist's Brush

When leaves begin turning golden, rust and red –
We wonder and marvel at this –
This from the Artist's Brush.

A large tree, outside my window,
bursts into a brilliant gold –
Causing its trunk, limbs and branches to turn ebony.
Accomplished by the Artist's Brush.

An old covered bridge – it's sides slit,
allowing autumn's colored leaves
To cover its long narrow path.
Colors from the brush of the Artist.

A lake surrounded with bright yellow leaves,
from tall white barked majestic Aspen,
these were painted by the brush of the Artist.

Kids jumping into huge piles of multi-colored leaves –
All painted by the brush of the Artist.

The Artist is able to do this – year after year after year!

Joys Of Love

When someone you love, loves you
in return,
feelings so warm and deep that you
cannot earn.
Gentle touches given in moments
of pleasure.
These joys of love, I shall
always treasure.